A PLEA
AGAINST
EXTREMISM

The views of Calvin, Hodge and others on some aspects
of the Roman Catholic Church

John Tallach

Christian Focus Publications Ltd

*For all the law is fulfilled in
one word, even in this; Thou
shalt love thy neighbour as thyself.
But if ye bite and devour one
another, take heed that ye be not
consumed one of another.*

Galatians 5:14–15

Published by

Christian Focus Publications Ltd

Tain	Houston
Ross-shire	Texas
Scotland	USA

© 1989

ISBN 1871676 11 8

Several people contributed substantially to the content of this pamphlet. Others showed their support by contributing to the project financially. To all who helped in any way the author would like to express his sincere thanks.

Contents

A PLEA
AGAINST
EXTREMISM

PREFACE

This pamphlet is largely based on Chapter 12 of the book by
Charles Hodge, *The Church and its Polity*.

Charles Hodge (1797–1878) has been described as *the* leading
American theologian of the 19th century. He was Professor of
Theology at Princeton Theological Seminary. Many readers
will be acquainted with his popular work *The Way of Life*,
re-printed by the Banner of Truth Trust in 1959. But some will
also be aware of his 3 vol. *Systematic Theology*. Along with his
lecturing and his other writings, this massive work established
Hodge's reputation as a theological leader, not only in America
but also throughout the Reformed Church around the world.

Some of the background to Hodge's treatment of the issues
raised in this pamphlet is as follows:

The General Assembly of the church to which Hodge
belonged[1] discussed in 1845 the validity of baptism administered by a Roman Catholic priest. The Assembly decided
against accepting the validity of such a baptism. Hodge felt
"almost overwhelmed" by this decision. He was particularly
alarmed at the haste with which such an important issue had
been raised and responded to. He felt sure that the Church as a
whole had not given serious consideration either to the issue or
to its implications. He wrote to express his dismay, and to plead
with his church to think more deeply before departing from a
position adhered to by the Reformers, and by the Reformed
Church since their day.

---

1 The Presbyterian Church in the U.S.A.

As far as my particular denomination[2] is concerned, there is abundant evidence identifying it with the views set out by Hodge. Revs Neil Cameron, Neil MacIntyre and Donald Beaton accepted this position. More recently, Rev D. A. Macfarlane spoke at a Theological Conference in support of it.

Hodge's position has also been followed in the practice of the F.P. Church. At least one person held office and at least one still does, who were baptised in the R.C. Church. One Italian gentleman, born and baptised in the R.C. Church, was received into membership in London when the late Rev J. P. MacQueen was minister there. Also, two Italian ladies became members of the Church in Glasgow during the earlier part of the ministry of the Rev D. Maclean. Not one of these was re-baptised before being accepted into membership or office. The baptism they had received while still within the R.C. Church was accepted as valid in each case.

The front cover, for obvious reasons, features Charles Hodge. It also features John Calvin because his influence pervaded Hodge's writings, as it does also the material presented here. It is not too much to say, I believe, that this plea against extremism is their plea.

18 Carlton Place
Aberdeen

John Tallach
April, 1989

---

2   The Free Presbyterian Church of Scotland.

PRELIMINARY POINTS

(a) Although Hodge pled with his church not to adopt an extreme attitude, he did not wish his pleas for moderation to be misunderstood. He did not wish his warning to be interpreted as implying the least shred of sympathy towards the many errors of the Roman Catholic system.

(b) However abhorrent the errors of the Roman Catholic system were, Hodge believed that a blanket denunciation of everything associated with the Roman Catholic Church was to be discouraged. "The cause of Protestantism suffers materially from the undiscriminating denunciations heaped upon the Church of Rome, and from transferring the abhorrence due to her corruptions to her whole complicated system of truth and error."

(c) Hodge takes some of the heat out of the debate when he places it within the context of the whole history of the Christian Church. The Early Church, too, had to decide on the validity of baptism carried out by groups holding unscriptural views. So, long before the Reformation, the leaders of the Christian Church adopted a settled view on this question. Their decision was that, whatever heretical views were held by a particular group, the baptisms carried out by them were valid, provided they were performed in the name of the Father, the Son and the Holy Ghost.

THE MAIN ISSUE

(a) *Three Essential Elements*

Hodge begins his discussion by quoting the answer to the question in the Shorter Catechism "What is baptism?". From the answer to this question, he picks out three elements which are essential to the Westminster Assembly's definition of baptism.

(i) There is washing with water. (ii) This washing with water must be carried out in the name of the Trinity. (iii) The washing with water in the name of the Trinity must be with the "professed ostensible intention of complying with the command of Christ, and of doing what he requires to be done by those who accept the covenant of grace."

(b) *Does Roman Catholic baptism include these essential elements?*

Hodge then goes on to discuss whether or not all these elements which he has drawn out of the Shorter Catechism definition are present in the baptisms administered by the Roman Catholic Church.

(i)   It is water which is used.

(ii) It is water administered in the name of the Trinity. Hodge quotes from the Council of Trent to show that, in this respect "The form is identical with our own".

(iii) In the teaching of both Protestants and Roman Catholics the design of the sacrament is that "by baptism, we are formally constituted members of the visible church and partakers of its benefits." Hodge freely admits that, in certain respects, there are great differences. The R.C. Church teaches that baptism is essential to salvation and that, when administered to infants, it uniformly secures salvation. However, he does not accept that these differences invalidate the ordinance, as administered in the R.C. Church. "It is out of all reason to say that the rite is valid if it is supposed to be effectual to some at an indefinite time: and invalid if supposed to be always effectual when there is no opposition."

Thus the three essential elements in the Shorter Catechism definition are present in baptism as carried out by the R.C. Church: "We have now shown that Romish baptism fulfils all the conditions of valid baptism, as given in our standards. It is a washing with water in the name of the Trinity, with the ostensible and professed design of making the recipient a member of the visible Church, and a partaker of its benefits."

DISCUSSING SOME DIFFICULTIES

Hodge then goes on to discuss some objections which have been raised to the position which he believes he has established on the basis of the Shorter Catechism.

(a) *Is baptism administered within the R.C. Church invalid because that church is not part of the visible Christian church?*

Hodge is as concerned as anyone to maintain the purity of the church. However, he warns against an imbalance creeping in here. "The course commonly pursued is to give a definition of a pure church, and then to declare any community not embraced in that definition to be no church. Thus it is said, a church is a congregation of believers in which the pure word of God is preached; the pure word of God is not preached in Rome, therefore Rome is not a church. By the same argument the whole world may be unchurched, save our own particular sect, no matter how narrow that sect may be. This method of reasoning is just as unreasonable as it would be to say, a Christian is one who believes the doctrines and obeys the precepts of Christ, therefore no man who is erroneous in doctrine or practice can be a Christian; which would be to go beyond even Perfectionists, for they do not make a perfect faith essential to the character of a Christian. We cannot take a definition of a perfect Christian as the rule of decision whether any particular man is to be treated as a brother; nor can we take the definition of a pure church as the criterion of the being of a church."

What, then, is to be the basis on which we approach the question of whether or not to accept a particular church as part of the visible church? Hodge says that "If we deny to any body of men the character of a church, on account of its creed, we thereby assert that no man holding that creed can be saved. To determine, therefore, whether a man or a church is to be denied the Christian character, we must ascertain what is the minimum of truth that can save the soul. For to deny that a man is a Christian on account of his ignorance or errors, and yet admit he may be saved, is to contradict ourselves. And to say that a

6

body of such men is no church, is no less a contradiction. It is therefore evident that the question, What is a true Church? resolves itself into this: How little truth may avail to salvation?" His conclusion is, "Any man who professes truth enough to save his soul is not to be denounced as no Christian, simply for his faith's sake. And any body of men that professes truth enough to save men cannot, on the ground of heresy, be denied the character of a church." Later on he expresses this positively: "Any religious body in communion with which men may be saved is a part of the visible church."

The question remains, What happens when we apply this test to the R.C. Church? Hodge warns that care is needed as to how we use the term "church". In this context, he says, we must not think of it in the sense of a particular organization which, in the details of its teaching, stands apart from all other organizations. Here, we must take "church" much more basically. We must take it simply in the sense of a collection of people who profess saving truth. Hodge goes on to list some of the saving truths which Roman Catholics profess. "They retain the doctrine of the incarnation which we know from the infallible word of God as a life-giving doctrine. They retain the whole doctrine of the Trinity. They teach the doctrine of atonement far more fully and accurately than multitudes of professedly orthodox Protestants. They hold a much higher doctrine, as to the necessity of divine influence, than prevails among many whom we recognize as Christians. They believe in the forgiveness of sins, the resurrection of the body, and an eternal life and judgement. These doctrines are in their creeds and, however, they may be perverted and overlaid, still as general propositions they are affirmed."

Hodge rejoiced that, in the record of its discussion, the Assembly of his church freely admitted that there are true believers in the Church of Rome. But he saw, as the Assembly apparently did not, that this lends support to the view that the R.C. Church must be seen as part of the visible church. How can the R.C. Church not retain enough truth to save the soul, if it contains true believers who have had no other means of instruction than what was available to them in that church?

How, then, can that be written off as no church which retains sufficient truth for the salvation of these souls?

(b) *Is baptism within the R.C. Church invalid because the priest is not "a minister of the word lawfully ordained"?*[3]

In approaching this question, Hodge again warns against the careless use of terms. Some people use the term "valid" as equivalent to regular, and "invalid" as equivalent to irregular. "But when Romish baptism is pronounced invalid, it is not declared simply irregular . . . It is said not to avail to the end for which baptism was instituted; it does not avail to make the recipient a professing Christian. Though a sincere believer should be baptised by a Romanist, such baptism would not signify or seal to him the benefits of the new covenant, nor express his purpose to obey Christ."

Hodge then goes on to make two points:

(i) Although the Confession does say that baptism should only be dispensed by a "minister of the Word lawfully ordained," the Westminster divines did not go so far as to include this in their definition of baptism, given in the Catechisms. Hodge is saying that, even supposing a priest did not qualify as "a minister of the Word lawfully ordained," that in itself would not render invalid baptisms administered by him. To say that the status of the person administering the sacrament was absolutely essential to the validity of the sacrament would be to go beyond the requirements laid down in the Catechisms.

(ii) But Hodge, in fact, goes on to argue that an R.C. priest can be regarded as meeting the requirements set in the Confession. "According to the common doctrine of Protestants," he says, "an ordained minister is a man appointed to perform the sacred functions of teaching and administering the sacraments in any community professing Christianity. . . . Do, then the Romish priests come within this wide definition of ordained ministers? Are they appointed by public authority to teach the Christian religion, and to

3 West. Conf. of Faith, chap. 27, sect. IV.

8

administer its ordinances? The question is not whether they are good men . . . or whether they are correct in doctrine; but simply, whether in a body professing to hold saving doctrine, they are appointed and recognized as Presbyters? If so, then they are ministers within the sense of the received Protestant definition of the term. The only ground on which this can be denied is, that they do not in any sense profess the Christian religion any more than Jews or Pagans."

(c) *If 2nd Thess. 2: 3-4 applies to the Pope, so that he is the Antichrist as the Confession teaches,[4] how can baptism administered within the R.C. Church be regarded as Christian baptism?*

Before a response is offered, a distinction has to be made. The Confession does not say that the Roman Catholic Church is Antichrist. It is the Pope who is Antichrist. We must distinguish between, on the one hand, the body of people within the R.C. Church who profess the Christian faith and, on the other, the papal and hierarchical system which has so largely perverted the people belonging to that church, and subverted them for its own ends. "The terms Antichrist, synagogue of Satan, etc., refer not to the mass of the people, nor to the presbyters of that communion, nor to the word of God, nor the saving truths which they profess, but to the Popish hierarchy and its corruptions. That hierarchy, with its usurpations and errors, is the mystery of iniquity, the man of sin, which in the church catholic, the temple of God, exalts itself above all that is called God, or that is worshipped. If Roman Catholics are no part of the visible church, then the Romish hierarchy is not 'the man of sin' spoken of by the apostle, for he was to rise and rule in the church. It is, therefore, one thing to denounce the Romish system and another to say that Romanists are no part of the church catholic."

This distinction has to be pressed in three ways.
(i)   When baptism is administered, it is not administered in the name of a particular denomination, but in the name of

4 Chap. 25, sect. VI.

9

Father, Son and Holy Ghost. A person professing the Christian faith is not baptised into a particular denomination, but into the visible church. It is wrong to think, therefore, that a person baptised within the R.C. Church is "baptised into a profession of all the heresies of popery".

(ii) If Protestants smear the whole Roman Catholic Church with the term "Antichrist," if they denounce everything to do with the denomination, they put themselves in an impossible position. How can we denounce as Antichrist those saving truths which we admit to be there? How can we disown as Antichrist those within the R.C. Church whom God calls to himself and whom we therefore have a duty to receive? "We shall sin against God and our own best interests, if we reject as reprobates any of the real followers of Christ, no matter in what external communion they may be found."

(iii) It may surprise us, but in fact if we refuse to distinguish between the Papacy and the R.C. Church, we put ourselves in the position where we cannot apply 2 Thess. 2: 3-4 to the Pope in the way that the Confession does. In that passage, the man of sin appears "in the temple of God". Surely the temple points to the church of God.[5] This is the subtlety of the mystery of iniquity. If it appeared outside the church, it would be much easier to denounce it, to warn against it. It is precisely because it appears within the church that it is able to do so much damage. But if the Papacy is the man of sin who appears within the church, it is impossible then to write off the church in which the Papacy appears as being no part of the church.[6]

5 1 Cor. 3: 16; Ephes. 2: 21, 22.
6 Calvin writes in a way which implies acceptance of this argument in the *Institutes*, Book IV, chap. II, sect. 12.

10

THE VIEWS OF THE REFORMERS, AND OF THE REFORMED CHURCH

(a) *On the validity of baptism administered within the R.C. Church*

Calvin gives a clear statement of his position in the *Institutes*, Book IV, chapter XV, section 16:

"If we have rightly determined that a sacrament is not to be estimated by the hand of him by whom it is administered, but is to be received as from the hand of God himself, from whom it undoubtedly proceeded, we may hence infer that its dignity neither gains nor loses by the administrator. And, just as among men, when a letter has been sent, if the hand and seal is recognised, it is not of the least consequence who or what the messenger was; so it ought to be sufficient for us to recognise the hand and seal of our Lord in his sacraments, let the administrator be who he may. This confutes the error of the Donatists, who measured the efficacy and worth of the sacrament by the dignity of the minister. Such in the present day are our Catabaptists, who deny that we are duly baptised, because we were baptised in the Papacy by wicked men and idolaters; hence they furiously insist on anabaptism. Against these absurdities we shall be sufficiently fortified if we reflect that by baptism we were initiated not into the name of any man, but into the name of the Father, and the Son, and the Holy Spirit; and, therefore, that baptism is not of man, but of God, by whomsoever it may have been administered. Be it that those who baptised us were most ignorant of God and all piety, or were despisers, still they did not baptise us into a fellowship with their ignorance or sacrilege, but into the faith of Jesus Christ, because the name which they invoked was not their own but God's, nor did they baptise into any other name. But if baptism was of God, it certainly included in it the promise of forgiveness of sin, mortification of the flesh, quickening of the Spirit, and communion with Christ. Thus it did not harm the Jews that they were circumcised by impure and apostate priests. It did not nullify the symbol so as to make it necessary to repeat it. It was enough to return to its genuine origin. The

11

objection that baptism ought to be celebrated in the assembly of the godly, does not prove that it loses its whole efficacy because it is partly defective. When we show what ought to be done to keep baptism pure and free from every taint, we do not abolish the institution of God though idolators may corrupt it. Circumcision was anciently vitiated by many superstitutions, and yet ceased not to be regarded as a symbol of grace; nor did Josiah and Hezekiah, when they assembled out of all Israel those who had revolted from God, call them to be circumcised anew."

Hodge quotes from this passage, and also from a submission presented by Calvin to the National Synod in the year before he died. In that submission Calvin argued that, despite all the corruptions found among the priesthood, "Roman baptism is founded upon the institution of Christ".

Baptism carried out by a priest was similarly declared valid in the Book of Discipline of the French Church. The French Synod of 1581 said of baptism performed by priests "since authority to baptise belongs to them according to the order of the Romish Church, baptism administered by them is not to be repeated."

In the passage from the *Institutes*, quoted above, Calvin refers to anabaptism. Anabaptists, as their name indicates, believed that those who had been baptised in the R.C. Church should be baptised again when they joined a Protestant church. All the Reformers distanced themselves from the Anabaptists, Luther being particularly outspoken in his denunciation of them. Knox similarly "repudiated the Anabaptists' insistence on the need for a new baptism".[7]

What was the view of the Reformed Church in the century after Calvin? Hodge quotes from Turretin, Professor of Theology at Geneva, who wrote that the Roman Church retains "the essentials of the ordinance and the true doctrine of the Trinity," though it "errs as to other doctrines".[8] The view in Scotland, expressed by Samuel Rutherford, was: "In a church that is no

7 R. P. Greaves in chap. 5 of his book, *Theology and Revolution in the Scottish Reformation.*

12

church there cannot be a true seal of God's covenant. But in the Court of Rome there is true baptism; for we baptise not again children once baptised therein."[9]

Summarising, Hodge supports his position by reference to the Reformed churches in Switzerland, France, Holland, Germany and England. He concludes that baptism administered within the R.C. Church "has been received as valid by all the Protestant churches from the Reformation to the present day".

(b) On the recognition of the R.C. Church as part of the visible Christian church

Of course, Calvin rejects the claims of the R.C. Church to be the only Christian church. He writes, however, "In the present day we deny not to the Papists those vestiges of a church which the Lord has allowed to remain among them amid the dissipation . . . Having deposited his covenant in Gaul, Italy, Germany, Spain and England when these countries were oppressed by the tyranny of Antichrist, he, in order that his covenant might remain inviolable, first preserved baptism there as an evidence of the covenant; baptism which, consecrated by his lips, retains its power in spite of human depravity; secondly, he provided by his providence that there should be other remains also to prevent the church from utterly perishing. But as in pulling down buildings the foundations and ruins are often permitted to remain, so he did not suffer Antichrist either to subvert his church from its foundation, or to level it with the ground . . . but was pleased that amid the devastation the edifice should remain, though half in ruins."[10]

In support of this approach, Calvin repeatedly draws a parallel between the R.C. Church and the church as it was during some periods of the Old Testament era. At such times there was the most wide-spread corruption, yet for all that the church did not totally cease to function as the church of God.

Summarising Calvin's position, he refuses to give the title of

8   Turretin was one of the most influential exponents of Calvin's thought. His 4 vol *Works* provided the basis from which, in former days in the F.P. Church, divinity students received their instruction in theology.
9   *A Peaceable, Temperate Plea for Paul's Presbytery in Scotland*, chap. 10 (p. 129).
10 The *Institutes*, Book IV, chap. II, sect. 11.

church in an unqualified way to the R.C. Church because this would obscure the fact that the R.C. Church is grossly defective in some respects. However, Calvin states that the foundation and the remnants of the Christian church are to be found in the R.C. Church; there are true believers there; and there are within it individual churches which he would call true churches.

Before leaving the Reformers, I wonder if we appreciate how seriously these questions affect them personally. If it is correct to say that R.C. baptism is invalid, the Reformers themselves were never baptised. If it is correct to say that the R.C. Church is no part of the visible Christian church, then the Reformers were never ordained to office in the Christian church. The views which Hodge is opposing are views which would put the Reformers out of office, and even out of the Christian church altogether.

Like Calvin, Turretin will not grant the title of church to the R.C. Church without qualification. How he describes the R.C. Church depends on the perspective from which he views it. Turretin states, however, "We admit the Church of Rome to be a Christian church in three respects: 1) In respect to the people of God, the elect, still remaining in it, who are commanded to come out. 2) In respect to the external form, in which we discover some of the elements of a church; in respect as well to the word of God and its preaching which, though corrupted, still remain; and as to the administration of the sacraments, especially baptism which, as to the substance, still remains entire. 3) As to Christian and evangelical doctrines, as concerning the Trinity, Christ as mediator, his incarnation, death and resurrection, and others by which she is distinguished from pagans and infidels."[11]

Discussing what constitutes the essence of the Christian church, James Bannerman quotes a saying in Latin which he supports by referring to the writings of the Fathers: "Where the true faith is, there the church is". As to whether or not the true

11 *Works*, vol. 3, p. 135.

faith can be found in the R.C. Church, the following extract from pp 21-22 of *The Full Harvest* makes clear what C. H. Spurgeon thought.

"In Brussels, I heard a good sermon in a Romish church. The place was crowded with people, many of them standing, though they might have had a seat for a halfpenny or a farthing; and I stood, too; and the good priest — for I believe he is a good man — preached the Lord Jesus with all his might. He spoke of the love of Christ, so that I, a very poor hand at the French language, could fully understand him, and my heart kept beating within me as he told of the beauties of Christ and the preciousness of His blood, and of His power to save the chief of sinners. He did not say, 'justification by faith,' but he did say, 'efficacy of the blood,' which comes to very much the same thing. He did not tell us we were saved by grace, and not by our works; but he did say that all the works of men were less than nothing when brought into competition with the blood of Christ, and that the blood of Jesus alone could save. True, there were objectionable sentences, as naturally there must be in a discourse delivered under such circumstances; but I could have gone to the preacher, and have said to him, 'Brother, you have spoken the truth;' and if I had been handling his text, I must have treated it in the same way that he did, if I could have done it as well. I was pleased to find my own opinion verified, in his case, that there are, even in the apostate church, some who cleave unto the Lord — some sparks of heavenly fire that flicker amidst the rubbish of old superstitution, some lights that are not blown out, even by the strong wind of Popery, but still cast a feeble gleam across the waters sufficient to guide the soul to the rock Christ Jesus."

CONCLUSION

The view that the R.C. Church forms no part of the Christian church and that baptism performed within it is to be disregarded as invalid was, for Hodge, a view in conflict with the Scriptures and with the Confession of Faith. It was also "at variance with all previously adopted principles and usage" in the Reformed Church; "in opposition to the principles of the whole Protestant world".

Hodge believed, to use again the words quoted near the beginning of this pamphlet, that "the cause of Protestantism suffers materially from the undiscriminating denunciations heaped upon the Church of Rome, and from transferring the abhorrence due to her corruptions to her whole complicated system of truth and error." In fact, ironically, he felt that those who fanatically distanced themselves from *everything* connected with the R.C. Church were to some extent showing the spirit of Popery themselves.

Hodge was alarmed as he wondered where this movement was leading — the movement begun by those who had got the Assembly of his church to pronounce Romish baptism invalid. He thought that, if applied consistently to other defective churches, these attitudes would lead to the point where "we shall have to unchurch almost the whole Christian world: and the Presbyterians, instead of being the most catholic of churches, admitting the being of a church wherever we see the fruits of the Spirit, would become one of the narrowest and most bigotted of sects."

What could Hodge do? He could remind his church of its real heritage; he could warn his church against the influence of those who were in fact destined to become increasingly extreme. Something of the depth of feeling which he brought to this task comes across in the words with which this plea against extremism comes to a close:

What new light has been discovered? What stern necessity has induced the Assembly to pronounce Calvin, Luther and all the men of that generation — as well as thousands who, with no other than Romish baptism, have since been received into the Protestant churches — to have lived and died unbaptised?

16

APPENDIX 1

Is it ever permissible for a sincere Protestant to attend Mass?
— what did Calvin say?

This Appendix is based on Calvin's tract "On shunning the unlawful rites of the ungodly, and preserving the purity of the Christian religion" (Calvin's Selected Works Vol. 3, part 3; pub. by Baker, 1983, pp 359-411).

Calvin originally wrote this tract as a letter to a friend in 1537. This man, like others at the time, found himself in an isolated situation, surrounded by those who had no sympathy for the Reformed Faith. He had written to Calvin to ask whether, though he did not agree with the Mass, he could continue to participate in it. Calvin's reply is an illuminating but complex piece of writing from a time when, for most, the Reformation was in its infancy.

Taking our lead from the title, we may read this tract with the assumption that we already know what Calvin's position is. We may even hurry through it, searching for the isolated quotation which seems to support a total ban on attendance at the Mass. But this is not something to be read in a hurry. We must go through it carefully, guarding against reading what *we think* into the words which Calvin uses.

To reinforce this warning, I would like at the outset to quote a comment from page 400. Calvin says that he does not want to be confused with "those absurd describers of religion . . . who make it wholly consist in merely abominating the Mass." Far from wishing to be associated with those people whose whole religion seemed to be negative and lacking in life, Calvin says "I think their error ought to be strenuously resisted". I would like to encourage careful thought about Calvin's actual position regarding attendance at the Mass by asking the following questions:

1. *What is the overall aim of the Calvin's tract?*
   Calvin repeatedly draws attention to the idolatry which is

17

involved in the celebration of the Mass. On the very first page he refers to "the Mass, that head of all abomination," in which "every imaginable kind of gross profanity is perpetrated". From this, as even from the title of the tract, it is perfectly clear that Calvin's general aim is to discourage attendance at the Mass.

2. *How should we view statements which may appear to place an absolute ban on attendance at the Mass?*

(a) "Come now," Calvin says on page 385, "and consider with me, in regard to a pretended observance of the Mass, with what kind of conscience you can be present at the performance of its mysteries?"

At first sight we might think from this that Calvin opposed attendance at the Mass, whatever the circumstances. However, we have to remember that Calvin's friend (whom he called Nicodemus) did not ask permission merely to attend Mass. He wanted to have full and frequent participation as well. In the course of the tract, Calvin repeatedly indicates that this is the specific question he is answering. On page 369 he speaks of images being "worshipped by bodily gestures;" On page 386 he says, "While all prostrate themselves . . . you prostrate yourself also".

Calvin lays it down as a general rule that Nicodemus cannot be present because, for various reasons, the conditions under which Nicodemus wants to be present are unacceptable.

(b) On page 387 Calvin says, ". . . I have long been maintaining on the strongest grounds that Christian men ought not even to be present at (the Mass)".

Calvin is here dealing with priests who professed to have embraced the Reformed Faith, but who wished so far to conceal their position as to continue officiating at the celebration of the Mass. Is it not possible, seeing Calvin was addressing men whose involvement in the R.C. Church had been so total, whose commitment to the Reformed Faith was still so weak, that he spoke to them with a firmness which took their special circumstances into account?

There are passages, then, where Calvin can appear to pronounce a ban on attendance at Mass. But there are also indications, in the immediate and the broader context in which these passages occur, that Calvin is dealing with particular cases.

One special reason why we must be careful when arguing from particular cases to a general rule will become more apparent in the second part of this Appendix. The evidence is clearly there that Calvin's attitude towards attendance at the Mass varied according to the circumstances of a case. If, on the basis of a ban which Calvin places in a specific case, we claim that Calvin banned attendance in an unqualified way, we make Calvin's position at one point in the tract inconsistent with his position elsewhere. If it is possible to interpret the tract as a whole in a way which avoids leaving one part of it in conflict with another, is it not reasonable and charitable to do so?

3. *What evidence is there that Calvin did not place an absolute ban on attendance at the Mass?*
   (a) Calvin makes it plain that it is not just presence at the Mass which is to be considered. The important factor is the *motive* of the person who is present. "I hold that we must not merely consider what attendance at the Mass is when viewed by itself, but what weight is to be given to it when taken in connection with its circumstances. My opinion is that this weight is exactly proportioned to the concession which they mean to make to the unjust demands of the ungodly" (page 398). Calvin says that the degree to which he is opposed to attendance is exactly proportional to the degree to which such attend-

ance is intended to conceal the individual's commitment to the gospel. It is evident that, where such a motive is missing, Calvin's attitude to attendance is quite different.

(b) Towards the close of his letter, Calvin shows a sensitivity towards his friend's position, and a degree of flexibility regarding it. He knew that, if Nicodemus would completely cut himself off from the official Church in his area, the R.C. majority who attended it would misunderstand. They would take it that Nicodemus was completely turning his back on God. Calvin advised that, to avoid this "suspicion of impiety," Nicodemus should occasionally "appear at their sacred meetings" (page 407).

Calvin went on to give another warning against an extreme approach. "Unless you are preparing to give anyone an exposition of your faith," he said, "indulge their bigotry so far as not to push yourself forward at the time when they are performing their rites, causelessly to make a display of contempt, which you are aware that they (such is their ignorance) will regard as sheer impiety against God" (page 407).

For the question even to arise as to Nicodemus pushing his way forward to raise a protest against these idolatrous rites, the assumption is that he is present at them.

(c) In advising that Nicodemus "seldom appear at their sacred meetings," Calvin was addressing someone who had not yet openly rejected idolatry. Where someone had publicly rejected idolatry, it was even more clear that their attendance at idolatrous worship did not, in itself, bring guilt on the conscience.

This emerges during Calvin's discussion of Naaman (2 Kings 5:18), who asked permission from Elisha to accompany his king when he went to worship the Syrian god Rimmon. Calvin does not want Nicodemus to use the example of Naaman in support of his case for participation in the Mass. But as far as Naaman's presence in the heathen temple was concerned, Calvin felt that this presented no difficulty. Naaman was not engaging, nor pretending to engage, in idolatrous worship. He was in the heathen temple as the servant of his sovereign and his prior, public profession of faith in the God of Israel prevented his presence in the house of Rimmon from giving basis for suspicion that he had any sympathy towards idolatry.

(d) It is at this stage in the tract that Calvin sets out his position most systematically. "I think I correctly define the proper limit when I say that you are utterly to abstain from all fellowship with any form of sacrilege, meaning by fellowship not mere proximity of place (which cannot be considered as connection) but inward consent, and some kind of outward manifestation indicative of consent" (page 394). There are two main points here:

(i) The important question is, the spiritual relationship between the individual and whatever idolatrous worship is in question. The believers to whom Calvin was writing still betrayed a weakness for idolatrous worship, a willingness to become personally involved when they were present at it. Calvin, having a great pastoral burden for these people, was obviously concerned at the influence which the Mass continued to exercise over them. That is one reason why, in general, the thrust of his writing is towards putting as great a distance as possible between them and the Mass.

(ii) One does not incur guilt merely by standing close to idolatrous worship. Calvin dismisses as superstition the idea that pollution follows merely from our foot entering a temple, or our eye resting on an image (page 393). Calvin illustrates this point from the life of Paul. At Athens, Paul walked around "places which exhibited the traces of a thousand impieties, and still perhaps smelt of recent sacrifices" (page 394). This, Calvin says, Paul did "without injury to his piety". In fact, from what he says in this passage, Calvin regards it as a positive testimony to a man's relationship with God if he stands among idolatrous worshipppers and refuses to become involved in their idolatrous practices.

(e) Calvin obviously hoped that, through this tract, his readers would be stimulated towards a spiritual maturity to which they had not yet attained in 1537. He hoped that they would reach the stage where they were maintaining a consistent witness and were openly rejecting idolatry. He himself volunteered, when they would reach that stage, to hold another discussion with them. During that discussion they would consider together "how far I am to concede to them permission to be present at Mass, and other profane rights of the same nature, in the discharge of civil duty, as in attendance at the funerals of kindred, or the celebration of marriage" (page 403).

The prospect of such a discussion proves that Calvin did not, in this tract, place an absolute ban on attendance at the Mass.

APPENDIX 2

"Free Presbyterians and the Requiem Mass"

It is obvious that this Appendix would not have been written, but for the prior publication of the above book. I fully appreciate the delicacy of the situation which lies behind both the book and this Appendix. However, I feel that the dissemination of mis-information at such a critical time calls for at least some limited response.

1. *The book is untimely.*

   What the book does not say is that two of the three authors are the same persons who have made a complaint in connection with the very issues dealt with in the book, against a brother in the Church.

   Surely, if there was ever an appropriate time for issuing this book, it is **not** the period prior to the final hearing of this case by the supreme court of the Church. If the *sub judice* rule should restrain anyone, should it not particularly restrain those principally involved in pursuing a case?

2. *The book is confusing.*

   On page 33, the Rev D Maclean is quoted as saying that "there are many things in the Church of Rome with which we would agree; for instance, the Church of Rome teaches the doctrine of sin and a lost eternity, and that is not taught in many Churches in this land at the present time. The Church of Rome holds that the Bible is inspired . . ." Yet, in the Preface, the hope is expressed that the book will "concentrate people's minds on the utterly unchristian nature of Romanism". Are we being asked to regard the doctrines mentioned on page 33 as "utterly unchristian"? The book gives us no guidance as to how we are to clear up this confusion.

3. *The book is unreliable.*
    (a) On page 19, the book reports that:
    In a Synod Resolution on the Church of Rome, the 1966
    Synod stated: "Rome has struck at the mediatorial office
    of Christ. By its doctrine of the mass, it has dishonoured
    the devine sacrific of the Lamb of God." (*Proceedings of
    Synod, 1966*, pp 10-12).

    The first sentence quoted from the Synod Resolution
    did not, in fact, begin as represented in the book. The
    Synod Resolution reads, "*By its exaltation of the Virgin
    Mary* Rome has struck at the mediatorial office of
    Christ." The deletion of the first part of the sentence
    means that the Synod Resolution has been altered in the
    book so as to make the Mass predominate.

    (b) On page 25, the book quotes from the F.P. Magazine to
    show how President Wilson was criticised for attending
    a Mass in New York. The book then goes on, "Wilson is
    further strictured for sacrificing his religious principles
    on the altar of political expediency, *and for putting his
    calling in this world before the demands and obligations of
    Christ.*" (c.f., F.P.M., VOL. 18, p397).

    This appears to be a summary of what was originally said
    in the F.P. Magazine, but there is no basis for the
    section which I have picked out in italics. The authors of
    the book have inserted this themselves.

4. *The book is misleading.*

    (a) In various ways, the book claims to give the official
    position of the Free Presbyterian Church on the diffe-
    rent aspects of Roman Catholicism with which it deals.
    In fact, significant sections of the book represent no
    more than the personal opinions of individuals.

    (b) On page 7 it is suggested that acceptance of the R.C.
    Church as part of the Christian Church is a new idea. It
    is claimed that those who hold this view are ignorant,

have been influenced by Romish propaganda, and have succumbed to spiritual sleep.

In fact this view, which is presented as new and which is criticised so severely, has always been the view both of the Reformed Church in general and of the Free Presbyterian Church in particular.

(c) On page 50, the authors present Calvin as supporting a total ban on attendance at the Mass.

In fact, as has been shown in Appendix 1, there were circumstances in which Calvin did tolerate attendance at the Mass.

(d) On page 51 the claim is made that Calvin, along with other Reformers, believed that "the Roman Mass was a rite so profane that Christians could not attend it without a protest against it and for the true Christ".

This claim does not correspond with the passage from Calvin, quoted on page 20 of this pamphlet. There he advised his friend, when occasionally present at services involving idolatrous worship, "Indulge their bigotry so far as not to push yourself forward at the time when they are performing their rites, causelessly to make a display of contempt . . ."

(e) According to the book, there is a vital difference between attending a Roman Catholic funeral and attending a Mass. But the fact is that, to be present at a Roman Catholic funeral means to be present at a Mass.

5 *The book is irrelevant.*
   (a) The book contains many statements which rightly expose the idolatry which the Mass involves, these statements consisting largely of protests made at various points throughout the history of the Free Presbyterian

Church. To gather these together at this stage "for the especial information and instruction of the Free Presbyterian Church" (Preface) suggests that there is now some dispute on this issue within the Church.

But there is no dispute within the Church about the idolatry and other evils connected with the Mass.

(b) The protests listed were largely made against the actions of those whose commitment to the Reformed Faith was at best questionable. If we follow Calvin's view, we will regard the citing of such protests as irrelevant to the case of anyone who, like Naaman, has openly renounced idolatrous worship.